The Art Of Being Human

By Celinne Da Costa

Foreword

To all the dreamers:

Somewhere along the way, someone told you that the flame burning in your heart needs to be extinguished. To get back to reality and live the life that was prescribed to you.

But you kept dreaming, because you knew they were wrong. That's likely how this book found you.

This is a collection of short stories from a life-changing journey around the world—a journey that taught me that we are indeed capable of creating a life that we are proud of and manifesting our dreams into reality. The best part? We don't have to do it alone.

In chronological and geographical order, I share with you:

Unexpected lessons about love, freedom, and happiness from the wise humans I met during my travels

The beautiful cultural nuances that make different places on this planet special

Serendipitous and eye-opening moments that guided me along a path to self-discovery

Read one story every day, or read them all at once. It's up to you. Whatever you choose…

Keep dreaming.

Don't stop believing that there is more.

And remember that, when you let them, the people around you can help uncover the limitless oasis of joy, love, and possibility that exists within you.

The Nomad's Oasis:
A Journey That Changed Everything

In May of 2016, I embarked on a journey around the world that changed me in ways I could have never imagined.

By then, I was working in corporate America for three years, and I could feel my soul slowly wilting. Growing up as an Italian-Brazilian immigrant in the United States, I was sold the American Dream: work hard, make lots of money, buy a white-picket fence house in suburbia, retire and travel when I'm old.

For years, I followed the rules, acclimating to New England's homogeneous suburbs, attending an Ivy League university, and working my way up New York City's corporate ladder. I spent a better part of my teenage and young adult years hiding behind a mask of who I thought I was supposed to be, all the while believing there was something wrong with me for constantly questioning whether the path to happiness could really be paved with so many instructions.

One day, I decided it was time to change my life. A series of eerily timed events forced my eyes open to the reality that if I didn't do something, I would indefinitely remain stuck in someone else's dream. But what I wanted was to feel true happiness, to pursue my passions, and most importantly, to understand what it truly meant to be human. Desperate for change, I entertained a crazy thought. What if I designed a life that incorporated all my passions—writing, traveling, and connecting with others—and just started living it?

Six months later, I quit my advertising job, packed a carry-on, and set out to prove that I could circumnavigate the globe by exclusively staying with people with whom I shared a human connection. This meant that everyone who hosted me had to be personally connected to me somehow (friends, friends of friends, people I met on the road, etc).

I spent close to a year putting my fate into the hands of others–mostly strangers–around the world. An astonishing 70+ people in 20+ countries across five continents opened their homes to me. Not only that, they fed, nursed, encouraged, nurtured, and advised me; during our time together, they shared with me their wisdom, dreams, fears, and deepest insecurities.

I believe they did this because they recognized in me what they recognized in themselves: a hunger for life, and to do more with our days than just work, pay bills, and die. Regardless of race, culture, or socioeconomic background, every person I encountered along my travels generously offered me a piece of his or her self, and as a result, unlocked a love for humanity in me that I didn't even know existed.

What would life be like if we were aware of the tiny miracles that envelop our present moment? If we took a few minutes out of our day to listen– really listen–to somebody and realize that every single person on this planet has something valuable to teach us? What if we woke up every day with a shared appetite for life, experience, and adventure? What would it mean for us and for others, if we were able to pursue what set our souls on fire?

My journey taught me that we are indeed capable of changing and living our lives to the fullest, and we don't have to do it alone.

That's what this collection of short stories is about: when we listen to our heart and become active participants in our lives, the answers come... often from everyday people who are unaware of their own brilliance. From a stranger we meet in an airport to a passing conversation we had with a friend, these moments of connection bring with them the opportunity to uncover the oasis that exists within each one of us: that internal space that, when found, allows us to meet our kindred spirits, rediscover ourselves, and manifest our dreams.

In this book, you will find tales of the journey I've taken to become the architect of my own life, as well as curated bits of wisdom from people I encountered around the world who taught me that being human is an art, and this life is our canvas.

As I carve out my own path, unruly and winding as it may be, I hope I can lend you some inspiration to help build yours.

Love,

Celinne

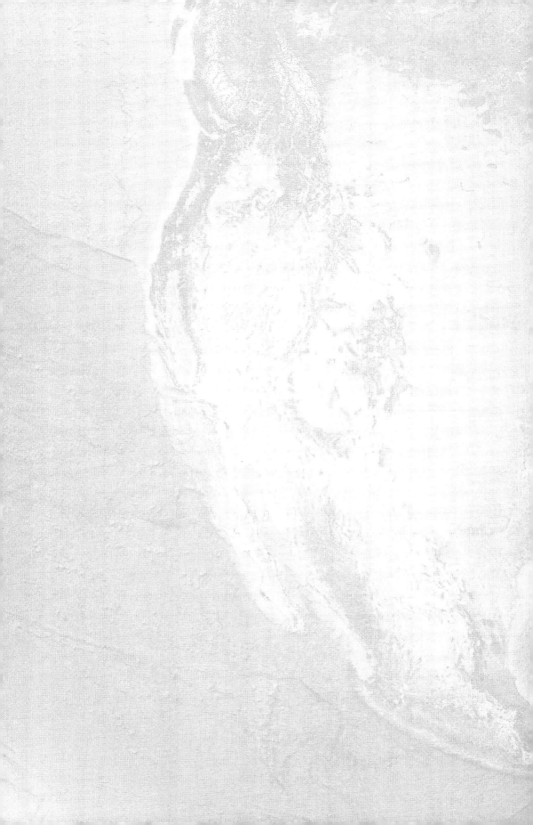

The Beginning:
USA

The Golden Glow Of Melancholy

[New York]

Today is my last day living in New York City.

In celebration, I sit watching the sunset from my window. How many hours I have spent sitting on my bed, gazing out from my little private corner of this city—a view so arresting, that in the time I've lived here I didn't dare put up curtains.

We leave a little piece of ourselves everywhere we go. This is mine: a collage of pastel sunrises and sunsets; a touch of melancholy bathed in the golden glow of the self that I discovered here.

Italy

On The Verge

You know that feeling when you're working really hard on something and are just on the verge of giving up–but don't want to?

This morning, I took a really difficult exercise class. We were doing a ton of abs by the end, and I was seriously struggling to push through. At one point, in the midst of what felt like my hundredth crunch (it wasn't), I allowed myself to collapse on my mat.

As I lay there, eyes closed in embarrassing defeat, I heard the words "Forza, forza! C'è la fai!", which translates to "Strength, strength! You can do it!"

I looked over to see the older gentleman next to me smiling in the midst of his own strenuous ab workout.

It's funny because when I gave up, I was so sure I didn't have the strength to keep going. But, the second he playfully uttered those words, I somehow found the motivation to push through.

The incident reminded me of the many times when I was on the verge of giving up on a goal, and just when I was ready to admit defeat.. someone showed up. Someone, whether a loved one or stranger, believed in me and told me to keep going. And, because of that support, I did.

This makes me wonder, what are the small ways we can help those around us during tough times? How can we be that quirky Italian gentleman encouraging a woman who ate far too much pasta since getting here and hasn't exercised in two weeks?

Giving someone the strength to overcome challenges may sometimes be as easy as just telling them to keep going. Why not try it?

Croatia

Have A Nice Life

[Dubrovnik]

Something strange happened to me today. After three hours of sleep and a long layover in Croatia, I decided to get a coffee. It was a small kiosk and there was no one in line, so I started chatting with the friendly barista.

After a bit, I left to catch my flight and bid him goodbye. To which he responded: "You're welcome. Have a nice life."

In my experience, when spoken, that phrase generally has a negative connotation. It is associated with "get lost" or an indifferent dismissal, yet this was not the case. This man spoke those words so sincerely, kindly, and genuinely that I didn't question for a second that he meant it.

He wished me a nice life.

It's funny how, in the age of social media, it's so easy to keep in contact. Throughout my travels, I've met people for minutes–minutes– and become Facebook friends with them. It is a way not to lose the connections I've made, albeit short and fleeting. It helps me feel as I haven't really lost that person forever, even if I will never see them again. It's almost like hoarding relationships in a digital attic, where only a selected few will be revisited again.

That's why I was curiously taken aback when this man bid me goodbye. It was final. It was kind. It was a "pleasure to meet you, and now we part ways." It strangely made me feel comforted and peaceful knowing that I had a pleasant interaction, and it had run its course.

Not everyone is meant to remain tethered to you. Some connections are best made and left behind. That doesn't make them less meaningful– the most special will always remain, perhaps gathering dust, but always delicately stored in your memory.

Sweden

Embrace Weakness

[Skinnskatteberg]

You often show the people that you meet the best sides of you. What happens when you expose them to the worst bits, right away?

Camping and doing hardcore outdoors stuff is completely out of my comfort zone. Even so, I still consistently do it to challenge myself.

I spent four days in the Swedish wilderness with three strangers. Right away, I had to live and share my days with them—in nature. Where I am at my most useless.

This was a jarring experience for me. I didn't have the fraction of the survival knowledge or capabilities that my companions did. All my shiny accolades and sexy resume didn't matter out here. I felt so vulnerable and weak. I was self-conscious. I was even a little insecure... all feelings that I don't experience that often.

The experience was a refreshing reminder that we are all "weak" at something—and we shouldn't be hard on ourselves for it. Feeling vulnerable is human. We are not invincible, and we will always meet people who are better than us at something.

Mastering all of life's skills is impossible; what we can do is accept our weaknesses and work on improving them without shame or judgment. Just do the best you can.

Romania

It Doesn't Have To Be Difficult

[Brasov]

The other day, I was speaking to my Romanian host about my newfound difficulties leaving a life I was comfortable with to travel on my own and put my fate in the hands of strangers. He said to me: "things are only hard when you believe they were supposed to be another way."

Consistently, I've found that resisting or pushing back on the natural flow of certain events or situations only makes things more complicated. While I am a huge believer in taking action every day to enact positive changes in our lives, I have also begun to understand that sometimes, acceptance may be the best course of action.

Life only feels difficult or unfair when you believe you should have been dealt a different set of cards. Change that belief… and you change your reality.

You are exactly where you need to be because the life you've lead up until this moment has taught you everything that you know. Don't swim against your circumstances–use them to your advantage.

Ironically, change begins when acceptance happens.

Greece

Go Deep

Why are we so afraid to get deep with one another?

What I find so refreshing about the Greeks is their natural inclination towards philosophy and self-exploration (much which is rooted in their rich history + culture, as well as growing up in an anarchic, chaotic, and unpredictable environment).

People here listen when you speak with them, and respond with thoughtfulness. I found many Greeks I spoke with to be mature beyond their years.

In Greece, I was repeatedly plunged into conversations about existentialism, the current state of humankind, and the meaning of love—the types of conversations that really open you up and push you to think.

This experience made me wish that more people could be open with one another, more eager to tackle the big questions in life.

How much more could we personally grow if we could share our fears, passions, and vulnerabilities, instead of typical small talk such as asking someone how the weather is?

What do you say—are there small ways that you can strive to make your daily connections deeper, and how?

It's Better To Dance

[Cyclades Islands]

One of my last nights in Greece, I was invited by the village I was staying in to celebrate the main restaurant's seasonal closing.

It was like something out of a movie: 20+ Greeks set up tables in the middle of the plaza for the feast, and within a couple hours, everyone was drunk and dancing to live folk music.

Before I knew it, I was getting pulled into the crowd, dancing like a maniac to steps I didn't even know. The joy was infectious.

In that moment, I stopped thinking. I just felt it: the sounds of music weaving with the clash of glasses being thrown against cobblestone, the synchronicity of sweaty, euphoric people in movement, the flow of a Universe suspended in time.

After I left the dance circle, out of breath from both movement and laughter, one of the locals came to sit next to me.

"How did that feel?" He asked playfully.

Speechless from the magic of the moment, all I could do was laugh.

He put a hand on my shoulder.

"You see?" he said, "It's better to dance than to understand how to dance."

His words rang profoundly in my soul. The richest experiences in our lives are the one we FEEL first-hand, rather than try to understand by reading about them or watching as a bystander.

I could make hypotheses and assumptions about the meaning of their dancing, but it was not until I joined in their moment of communal unity that I truly felt it.

A lesson learned: only when we allow ourselves to feel, will we really understand.

And what a joy it is to feel.

What Matters

[Cyclades Islands]

When was the last time you let yourself go in the moment?

One of my last nights in Greece, I was invited to a crazy Greek party that ended up with lots of glass smashing and drunk people dancing.

The first glass smash was an accident. One of the locals bumped into the feast tables during a dance circle, sending the glasses, plates, and utensils flying all over the plaza.

As people continued to dance, one of the restaurant's staff began picking everything up and placing it on a chair. While she was doing that, a dancing man came up and kicked the chair down, sending everything scattering again.

Seeing the horror on my face, one of the locals turned and said to me: "Don't worry, that's the restaurant owner."

I was stunned. Even the owner of the restaurant, who should have cared about his stuff being kicked around, let himself go in the midst of the feast's euphoria.

The local proceeded to tell me that in Greece, throwing your glass on the floor was a metaphor for transcending mortality: the glass symbolizes life, and willingly breaking it is a way to come to terms with death.

Once again, I was reminded that what makes life precious has nothing to do with the material world. A life lived to the fullest asks us to let go: of fears, inhibitions, the walls we build around ourselves every day.

To live in joy and create real connections with our fellow humans in the most precious moment we have... the present.

Live for what matters. Everything else is a luxury.

It's Not True

"When you think, it's not true."

These words were whispered in my ear by a local during my last night in Greece, as we watched dozens of drunk Greeks dance around the main village square in sheer euphoria and celebration.

As I usually do when I hear what I recognize as wisdom, I immediately wrote his words down, hoping to understand them later.

During the next week, the meaning of his initially cryptic words began to unfold.

It goes back to the ancient philosophical belief that your thoughts are not YOU: they are a product of your culture, upbringing, and environment. We are conditioned to think a certain way, and your thoughts can only have the meaning that you assign to them.

Whatever you choose to think and believe will shape the course of your life, and you can also choose to change that at any point.

His words reminded me:

1. Don't believe your thoughts. Trust your intuition.

2. We are in control of how we perceive and manifest our world.

3. Where your thoughts go, energy flows.

At any given point, what you think is true can be totally wrong—so why not choose your thoughts?

We can teach ourselves to think in ways that support and enrich our lives. That's the reality we create for ourselves.

What thoughts have you chosen to entertain that have enriched your life, and which have you abandoned?

Humans And Explosions

[Cyclades Islands]

"Humans like explosions," a Greek man said to me recently.

It's not a thought that ever crossed my mind before but… I kind of agree.

According to this local, humanity craves explosion as a way of catharsis—seeing chaos manifest in the physical world somehow helps release the tension and anxiety that so many of us hold inside.

We like to see things crash, burn, and blow up, even more so when it's in a "safe" and contained environment. Think about how hungrily we consume violence and aggression in the media nowadays. In a twisted way, the fear we are sold is almost exciting.

Perhaps we really are programmed to get a thrill out of explosion.

And this doesn't have to be a bad thing.

On one hand, we can choose to get our cathartic fix with mental junk food: watching the media talk about how the world is a horrible place, consuming movies that exude violence, being bystanders to the negative actions that we witness.

Or.

We can channel the pent-up energy into something positive. We can transform that internal unrest into a passion so ardent that it moves mountains. Tapping into that inherent human craving for explosion, we can use the love that lives inside each one of us to transform ourselves and the world we live in.

In other words…

Explode with your love. With your willpower. With your appetite for life.

Explode until everyone around you feels the tremor of your soul.

Nepal

Why Do You Believe?

One of the first things I noticed about Nepal is that it is a country of piety. People here are tremendously dedicated to their families, their gods, and their traditions. There is something intrinsically beautiful and special about the rituals that many people follow, which have been long lost in most of the West.

For example, my host's grandmother cleans the Hindu gods' statues in the prayer room every morning. The swamis at the meditation retreat I'm at wake up at 5:30 am to begin each day with an hour of meditation. When I visit the temples, people unashamedly kneel deeply in front of their idols in loving worship.

Today I was speaking to a swami about how everyone has their own method of worship, and how vastly it varies according to their personal beliefs. To which he responded so beautifully:

"Why do you believe? If you believe something, it means you don't know. That's why you believe."

He's right. We don't know what the ultimate truth is. So let us find something to believe in.

The Responsibility Of Freedom

[Kathmandu]

Freedom has been a large topic of discussion at my meditation retreat. There is a strong belief that we should all be free, i.e. have complete autonomy over our actions and decisions without being dictated by what society tells us is right or wrong. There is a flip side to freedom, though. If you are free, then you are responsible for your actions. There is no one to answer for you but yourself.

Responsibility can be a burden, and that's why some people only like the idea of freedom. They talk about it, yearn for it, and preach it. But, when you open the door to their cage, they stay. Sometimes, they even fight you if you try to help them out. Imprisonment has become their home—it's comfortable, it takes care of their basic needs, and keeps them placated.

Those who truly crave freedom, fly away the second you give them an opening to. We crave it so deeply that we will CREATE that opening before waiting around for someone to open the door for us. Once you've experienced the intoxication, exploration, ecstasy of freedom.... You simply cannot go back.

The guru stated it perfectly: "Once you've tasted the freedom of the sky, how could you return to being unaware of your wings?"

Prayer Flags

[Kathmandu]

As I was hiking up Champa Devi mountain near Kathmandu, I found rows and rows of prayer flags strung along the trees, a Buddhist tradition brought over from Tibet. It's crazy but also beautiful to think that people climb these heights (trust me, it is not an easy climb) in order to bless their families and countryside, as the cloth banners have to be hung from high places. These colorful prayer flags have (you guessed it!) Buddhist mantras written on them and are either blue, red, green, red, or yellow to represent the five elements.

Yet another quality I so admire about Nepal is how everything seems to have its purpose.

In a country that is so outwardly chaotic, there is a deep, spiritual order that stretches back thousands of years. It is not a gratuitous culture; even though some traditions may not initially make sense to the outsider, it all begins to unravel once you ask the right questions.

Peace In Chaos

[Kathmandu]

What I love about Nepal so far: it is chaotic, but in that chaos there is a peaceful order; the Nepalis have an admirable reverence for the holy, which so many of us in the West have lost touch with; their commitment to their families and communities is sacred—they find love in the everyday little actions that we in the West may perceive as overbearing, excessive, or intrusive.

But that's not even what my favorite part is. What I love most about Nepal is the people. From the moment I've stepped foot into this country, I've been taken care of. And I don't mean that in terms of housing, food, or needs—though that, too—but more so in terms of my heart.

Here, I feel... taken care of. Respected. Wanted. I got sick, and the Nepalis nurtured me back to health. I felt sad, and they kept me company. I took photos of them, and instead of shying away from the camera, they smiled. People have tried to rip me off, and they've run to my rescue.

I've always understood that this country vibrated on a different level spiritually, but it's more than that: kindness runs in the Nepalis' veins. And I am here, wading in it, hoping to bottle even a little of it to carry with me.

Everything That Begins, Must End

[Kathmandu]

Nepali artists painting at a thangka school in Bhaktapur. I learned two lovely lessons about thangkas and Buddhist beliefs in general. For those who don't know, thangka painting is an ancient Tibetan Buddhist tradition dating back thousands of years. The paintings are made on cotton and contain exquisite depictions of Buddhist teachings, with the most popular designs being mandalas, the cycle of life, and the path to enlightenment.

Anyway, the first lesson is that mandalas, one of the most famous designs, depict the three doors to nirvana: mind (what you think), speech (what you say), and body (action). According to Buddhist teachings, you must purify and master all three before attaining enlightenment. Learn to control how you think, because that will impact what you say; what you say shapes the world around you, and it influences you to take actions. What your body does with your speech–e.g. how your actions manifest into this world–ultimately determines what you make of your life.

Second lesson is, some monks spend hours and hours making these beautiful mandalas out of sand rather than paint. After working on them for days on end... they destroy their creation. They scoop up all the sand, put it in some sort of sacred baggie, and pour it into the river. If you saw photos of these intricate masterpieces you wouldn't believe that these people have the heart to just throw them away.

And in fact, that's not what they're doing. The action of taking apart this intricate art symbolizes the transience of life: it's beautiful, it's a masterpiece, but eventually it must end. By pouring it into the river, monks believe they are spreading peace and love into the world. Everything in life, after all, must end eventually. That's why it's so important for us to remain present for every second of it, and live every day with the acknowledgement that someday, we too could bring a little peace and love into the flow of this spectacular planet.

A Song Of Names

[Chitwan District]

Did you know that almost everyone's name in Nepal has a specific meaning? Most of Western names come from religion, meanings in different languages, and occasionally from our own words. But in Nepal, it is almost sure that when you are saying someone's name, you are also speaking a word in Nepali.

When I was staying at Barauli Community Homestay, every hut had a person's name. Mine was Dilmaya, which roughly translates to "love from the heart" (how amazing is it that this is even a word?!). Along my travels, I've met people whose names mean light, human, point at the center, gifted, and so on. My first question now when meeting locals is the meaning of their name. It's a fun game to play.

I think there is something so inherently unifying about the fact that every time Nepalis speak their language, they are singing a song of their own people's names. Every sentence is a string of identities, of people who may never meet yet are unified through expression. It's no wonder this country has such a strong sense of community, of coming together and helping one another in times of need.

How could people not feel lovingly connected, when their names are the very fiber that ties their language together?

Namaste

[Chitwan District]

There are what seems to be infinite amounts of rice paddies surrounding the villages near Chitwan National Park. This part of Nepal is so different from the city. It's effervescent green, the air smells sweet, and animals roam free around every corner. The people are nicer, more laid back (as you'd expect from someone who doesn't deal with city stress), and there are hardly any tourists.

It's been refreshing to be met with genuine curiosity and kindness—no one here is trying to sell me a tour or make some extra bucks off the foreigner. Most people cannot communicate with me, but they smile and wave. When we greet each other, we bow our heads, clasp our hands together, and say the Nepali salutation that I love so much: "Namaste."

I bow to the divine in you.

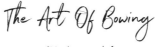

The Art Of Bowing

[Kathmandu]

A younger and more immature me used to scoff at people who incorporated bowing into their daily practice. I used to think, "why would I ever bow down to anyone? I'm my own person." I was wrong.

To bow is not a sign of weakness, nor must it have anything to do with religion. I've learned, especially in Southeast Asia, that the act of bowing is a practice of humility.

Bowing is a physical manifestation of surrender: a relinquishment of the ego, an acknowledgement of a force bigger than you at work, and an acceptance that ultimately, you are but a thread in this convoluted net of life that inhabits the planet.

Bowing is a sign of strength and respect towards the Universe. It is an exercise of opening the dusty chambers of a heart left darkened by a society that rewards individualism and selfishness. Open these chambers, every day, so that the winds of humility may dissolve the cobwebs woven from your judgments and preconceptions. Let the light in so that others may enter.

To bow is an act of universal love. And so I bow down to that greater force that exists not only around me, but within me.

The Body Burning

[Kathmandu]

Yesterday I witnessed a funeral at Pashupatinath Temple, a famous Hindu temple which for centuries has been located on the banks of the sacred Bagmati River (believed to be part of the holy Ganges River in India). It is also where many of Kathmandu's residents are cremated.

On one side of the river, bodies are burned in the presence of loved ones, and the ashes are then thrown into the holy water. The other side of the river is often used to celebrate one of Nepal's many festivals.

Standing in the middle of the bridge that connects these two sides was like balancing on a tightrope. One step forward, and I'd enter grief. One step backward, and I'd enter joy. For a moment, I hesitated crossing into the funeral side. I could almost feel the opposing winds of life and death pushing me into a perfect equilibrium.

We are constantly told that life is fleeting and that we are not invincible. It is one thing to hear about it, and wholly another to witness it. Watching a human body burn just a few meters for me was a profound experience. As I breathed in the thick, pungent smog of burning flesh and a dusty layer of human ash settled on my skin, it deeply sunk in just how fragile the human condition is.

Our magnificent bodies, these shells that carry us through our living experience on this earth, can so easily be rendered to nothing more than ash in a matter of hours. Ash that is then swiped into the river, diluted into minuscule particles of ourselves that will eventually disperse throughout the planet.

Body to ashes, ashes to dust. We come into this planet as specks; it is only natural that this is also how we must leave it.

Myanmar

Moments Of Self-Doubt

[Inle Lake]

Have you ever had those moments when you doubt yourself? When you think you're doing the right thing, you're pretty damn sure, but then those lapses come of "well, am I?"

That's how I feel sometimes about my decision to quit my life in New York City to "wing it" and attempt to carve out a path traveling full-time. Sometimes there are moments–often when I'm on crowded smelly buses for way more hours than I was told, yet another cab driver tried to rip me off, or I find myself in a remote village with no idea where I'm going– when I think, "what the hell were you thinking, Celinne?"

But then there are moments like these: when I'm cruising over a silky lake in the heart of Myanmar, listening to the harsh crackle of motor mixed with the soft swoosh of waves, feeling the wind's chill puckering my skin.

It is then that I think to myself: this is the most important thing in my life.

And of that I have no doubt.

The Graceful Resilience Of The Burmese

[Inle Lake]

A trait I've come to love about the Burmese in my past few weeks here is their graceful resilience.

I've heard some heartbreaking life stories from speaking to locals. Yet, what has really taken me aback is how nonchalant the Burmese are about their tragedies.

In Inle's villages, I met a woman who suffered from three almost full-term miscarriages due to working too hard on the field, before having a healthy fourth child. She told me this so casually that she might as well have been explaining that night's dinner. I also met a little girl who was born without fingers—when I waved at her, her mom held up her child's deformed hand, shrugged, and smiled apologetically as if to say "oops, sorry!". In Kalaw, I met a woman who lost her toddler after being failed by the medical system because she couldn't afford the necessary operation.

What shocks me is not that these people, who live in a third world country and under deplorable living conditions, have suffered more than I could fathom. What truly shocks me is the grace through which these stories are told: with a peaceful and calm acceptance that this is just the way life is sometimes.

I asked the Burmese woman who lost her toddler: "How can you smile so much and feel happy, after what you went through?" Calmly, she responded: "I understand that we all go."

That's it, isn't it? While we in the West treat every little problem like it's the end of the world, there are people who have suffered—really suffered—yet understand that in this world, we all go. And so we must keep going, pushing forward, smiling, loving, and practicing kindness. These beautiful people choose to smile despite what went wrong with their lives, and we can learn from that.

In the end, what defines us in life is what we choose to do with what we HAVE—not what we lack.

Freedom's Worth

[Inle Lake]

To anyone who's ever wondered why I strive to be free:

It's for moments like these. When I climb to the top of an ancient Bagan temple and feel the soft sunshine kiss my face as I overlook hundreds of years' worth of Burmese history and human achievement.

It's for when I take an 11 hour overnight bus to Inle Lake, get lost looking for the ferry, and have to find my way to my destination. And then, just as if the frustration never happened, I find myself in a little slice of heaven.

It's for when it is pouring rain, the electricity doesn't work, and there is no hot water, yet I simply don't mind because I am content with the balmy breeze enveloping my skin and listening to the sounds of the Ngapali ocean.

I live for this freedom because of the peace, tranquility, and love that it stirs within me. This feeling... it is always worth the hassle.

To anyone who's ever wondered why I strive to be free:

It's because it's brought me exactly to where I need to be.

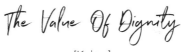

The Value Of Dignity

[Kalaw]

Today I was speaking with my Burmese guide, who lives in a remote village and has been working with tourists for a few years, and I asked her a semi-taboo question: "do you think that despite having so little, the people are happy?"

Her response made my heart hurt. Yes, they are happy, and even more so when they have foreign visitors.

"Why on earth would that be?" I asked. In my mind, I thought it was because of money.

To my surprise, her answer had nothing to do with that. She went on to explain that these communities are so poor and live in such terrible conditions that they feel ashamed. Wealthier people from their country never come to visit, and so it brings them joy when foreigners care enough to stop by and sit in their humble homes, drink their tea, and eat their food.

Foreigners bring their children candy, are willing to touch them by shaking their hand, and talk to them like fellow human beings—while so much of their own society shuns them for their poverty. What foreigners provide them with, other than the obvious financial relief, is dignity.

How is this is even a reality—that any of us can think we are better than someone just because they were born in less fortunate conditions? Those who are privileged are not special. They are lucky, and that luck should be shared with others. Not just with the countries we visit because it's cool and novel to experience their culture—but also within our own communities.

Everyone deserves to be seen and valued, no matter what their background is.

Trust And Fear Go Hand-In-Hand

[Mandalay]

The other day, my new friend and I met two local Burmese at a monastery who, after chatting for a couple of hours, offered to take us the next day to a remote waterfall about 50 km from Mandalay.

Without thinking twice about it, we agreed. The next day, we headed to a milky blue waterfall pool mostly frequented by locals, with the occasional tourist (you have no idea how many selfies I had to take with locals that day). The waterfall had two levels: an easily accessible one, and an arduous (and more beautiful) one that required climbing to the top of a mountain and going through some deep waters.

One of our new friends was afraid of swimming and got "stuck" in the part that required wading through deep waters. I offered to help him across, but he wouldn't budge. It wasn't until another local man came by and offered to help us that we were, in joint effort, able to get our friend across the water and to the other side. This local man continued to guide us to the more difficult waterfall. There was even one point when the waterfall was falling down so strongly, I had to completely close my eyes and let them guide me through the passageway. Eventually, we made it.

My lesson for that day? Trust and fear go hand in hand. When you trust—truly trust—you cannot fear. Likewise, when you fear, you cannot trust. If I hadn't trusted these locals, I would have never experienced this precious gem. If my new local friend hadn't trusted us, he may not have made it to the top. If I hadn't trusted the random man who led us there, I may not have made it either. If I didn't trust that I was capable of climbing those rocks, I would have missed out on a tremendously beautiful experience.

I've found that a life better lived is one where we constantly exercise trust, in others and ourselves. Who knows where that may lead you—it could be in the middle of the Burmese jungle, jumping into a turquoise natural pool with your new friends.

Communication Without Words

[Mandalay]

Last week, I was swimming in one of the natural pools in the waterfalls of Mandalay when two local girls joined me. They didn't speak English, but—as one does when clueless to a language while traveling abroad—we communicated in smiles.

We swam in harmony, occasionally exchanging giggles and squeals of glee. Some time passed, and the local girls swam past me on their way out. Before climbing onto the rocks, one of them turned around. She smiled warmly at me and spoke the first, and only, English words I'd hear from her: "Are you happy?"

It wasn't a "good-bye," or "how are you," or "see you later." She asked me the only questioned that really mattered.

I smiled back and said: "Yes."

Funny how much can be communicated in an exchange of only four words: in those 30 minutes together in the water, we spoke a language that carried no words. Isn't that understanding, after all, part of what happiness is?

The Little Things

[Bagan]

It's the little things.

It's when I'm biking down a pitch black dirt road—the only light coming from the phone awkwardly stuck in my bra—and rather than passing me, the car behind me drives slowly with its headlights on so I can see ahead. It's when locals offer to drive me and a friend two hours each way to show us an undiscovered place, and ask for nothing in return. It's when I get totally lost, end up in a restaurant full of locals, and the only two who speak English treat me to a delicious lunch—even though I can probably afford it more than them—and drive me back into town.

And these are only acts of kindness from the past week.

It's these little things that regularly remind me that humanity is good. That people are kind. That we can help each other, in little and big ways.

Each and every day is an opportunity to do something for someone else, however small it may be. Invest your kindness in others and do it indiscriminately. You never know when you may need someone to invest in you.

It Takes A Village

[Bagan]

The other day, I witnessed a group of young monks lining up for their daily ration of rice, served by fellow villagers. I asked my Burmese friend why that was, and when he told me what it's like to grow up as a monk in Myanmar, I was awed by the profound lessons in humility that children are taught at such a young age.

Many poor families, especially those afflicted by the past civil wars (and ongoing conflict), send their children at a very young age to monasteries to study and become monks. Monasteries are considered the best, safest places for children to grow up well and get an education in a poor and under-resourced country like Myanmar. When they turn 20, these kids can choose to reintegrate into normal life or become monks for life.

Every day, these little monks must go around the village to ask for donations of rice for their meal (except Saturday, when villagers go up to the monasteries to donate). This means every morning, there is someone waiting to provide for them.

Villagers take turns getting up very early to cook for the monks, so that they may have something to eat for their twice-daily meal at around 6 pm and 12 pm (they don't eat after that). How incredible is it that 1. these children are taught humility daily by having to depend on their community for nourishment and 2. that every day, the community pulls through and collectively chips in to help out the monks in their village?

I say this over and over again but I can't get tired of it: people are amazing.

Panda Love

As part of my project to couch-surf around the world through my social connections is that everywhere I go, I ask people from different countries, ethnicities, ages, and genders to answer the same five questions.

One of these questions is: "what does human connection mean to you?" I recently asked this to a 20-year-old Burmese student and his answer took me aback.

Human connection, he said, is driven by a feeling to take care of, love, and be kind to one another. People who feel this love in their heart want to help others simply because they are fellow humans, irrespective of race.

So, true human connection is all about cultivating that "panda" feeling. Panda feeling, you may ask? A panda, he explained, is white, black, chubby and Asian all in one. Even so, it is universally loved. When we have a "panda" feeling, we recognize that there are all kinds of different people existing in this world. Even so, we should accept them for who they are, because that's what humanity is: a little bit of everything. Humanity deserves to be loved for the awesomeness that it symbolizes collectively, and that love is all about giving, forgiving, and caring.

What makes special moments of human connection happen around the world, therefore, come from that panda feeling. So go out there, folks, and panda-feel the world.

A Love Affair

[Inle Lake]

They say you are your most ideal self when you are in love. That would explain why I am my most compassionate, open-minded, kind, and giving when I travel. .

I'm in love with how I can become completely vulnerable to strangers, spending hours on a beach in Myanmar exchanging life stories, heartbreaks, and our most intimate insecurities.

I'm in love with the sweet and utter bliss I feel when I'm riding on the back of a new friend's scooter in Greece, look up at a sky blanketed with twinkling stars, and think to myself: I've never felt so free.

I'm in love with how I can stay up all night writing and still have the stamina to wake up at the crack of dawn to see the sun rise over thousands of pagodas in Bagan.

I'm in love with seeing the sun set in each crevice of the world.

I'm in love with how each person I've befriended during my travels has contributed to assembling a piece of me.

I'm in love with how travel has taught me to let go... of frustrations, my fears, toxic people, and doubts.

I'm in love with how travel has expanded my heart—because the more I travel, the more I love.

Indonesia

When Change Comes, Flow

[Bali]

Today is my 26th birthday. Exactly one year ago, I spent my entire day choking back tears at a corporate New York City job I was utterly unsatisfied with, after being unexpectedly dumped the night prior by a man I wasn't crazy about.

At 25, I had big dreams, but I had settled. I worked for a company I didn't believe in, in a city whose lifestyle I didn't subscribe to, and indiscriminately dated people because I thought I should ("I mean, it's NYC, right?!"). I was content, but I was not living up to my potential. I was cruising by with a mediocre life and I was starting to accept it.

A series of events happened in the following months, as if by coincidence (but as we know, I don't believe in that), to push me over the edge. I got dumped, I didn't get promoted, my rent skyrocketed, and none of the jobs I was interviewing for in Europe felt like a good fit. The new year rang in and I found myself desperate and without a plan of escape.

That's when it hit me. When change comes, don't resist—flow. I decided that within 6 months, I would leave it all behind to travel around the globe by staying with people I knew and met through my social network. Rather than sit around and wait for my life to match my expectations, I would crowdsource my dream to travel the world by asking people who were connected to me for help.

I jumped into the abyss, with full faith that everyone in my network would be a thread to the net that would catch me. And here I am. Fourteen countries and 30+ hosts later, I've almost circumnavigated the globe purely through the power of human connection.

One year ago, my world began to fall apart. Today, I find myself in Bali having not only having picked up the pieces, but sharing them with anyone who wants to take part of my journey and help me arrange them into exactly the life I've wanted to live. I find myself celebrating another year of life with strangers-turned-friends from all over the world.

More importantly, I found me. And you know what? Me and my dreams... we are not going anywhere.

Happy 26 years of life to the person who's always had my back.

The Puppet Maker (Part 1)

[Jogjakarta]

There is something special brewing in the Javanese air. I've felt it from the moment I arrived to Jogjakarta. The people here are... delightfully, and notoriously, slow. They take their sweet time for just about anything: the concept of rush seems non-existent.

Which is ironic considering I just happened to meet a local Javanese guide when I was in a rush to get to the Jogjakarta palace. I arrived 30 min before closing, and this guide offered to show me around so that I could understand what I was seeing. Afterwards, he offered to take me around the city, which led into one of the most enlightened experiences I've had on this trip.

One of my stops was a shop that makes shadow puppets, a Javanese tradition dating back thousands of years. As I sat there, learning about the FASCINATING art of traditional puppet making (post coming on that later), I made conversation with the men there about Javanese culture and philosophy.

I learned that the Javanese don't like being in a hurry because to do something right, they feel that they must take their time. As one of them said "we must not do things quickly, but with feeling: if we allow time to control us, we cannot make something good. Time can pressure us but we cannot let it if we want to enjoy life."

And then, this man proceeded to tell me the secret to slowing down time and opening your heart to the Universe...

The Puppet Maker (Part 2)

[Jogjakarta]

I randomly found myself in a puppet maker's shop on Jogjakarta, and he proceeded to tell me the secret to slowing down time and opening your heart to the Universe.

After quietly listening to me speak with his colleagues about the art of puppet making, this man asked me what I wrote about during my travels. I told him that wherever I go, I look to capture the soul of that place and tell others about it.

To this, he responded: "When people are looking for soul, it means they have a strong mind." He had my attention.

He then proceeded to tell me that when the mind is too strong—a.k.a. when you think too much—it's not easy to open your heart because logic overrides your flow.

To treat my mind, then, I must "follow the feeling of the Universe." To which I thought...

What the hell does that mean?

It initially sounded like complete and total new age crap, until I learned that the Javanese define "feeling" in a completely different way. There is a specific word which the Javanese live by (it has no direct translation), which captures the essence of living in the moment and of savoring life's beauty.

That word is "rasa."

I spent the next two days learning the meaning of this word, and it is beautiful. What is rasa? Turn the page to find out…

Rasa

[East Java]

Rasa. Sitting in a puppet shop on a lazy Sunday afternoon in Java, I was introduced to the Indonesian concept of rasa when a wise puppet maker cryptically advised me to "follow the feeling of the Universe" in order to treat my overthinking mind.

The word in Indonesian roughly translates to "feeling," yet it also means taste. And, oddly enough, rasa translates to "juice" in Sanskrit.

When I later asked one of my hosts whether rasa referred to the juice of life, he laughed and responded: "it's more like the essence."

Rasa is feeling. It is essence, taste, juice. It can be happy, sad, good, or bad. Rasa is that indescribable internal commotion you get when you hear an exquisite piece of music. It's when you're standing on top of a mountain, overseeing the golden sunlight ripping through the morning fog down below. Rasa is the love that bubbles within you when a complete stranger spends the entire day showing you around simply because he believes in your dreams.

The cure to opening your heart and slowing down time, said the puppet maker, is to turn off your mind and feel the Universe. Rasa. Stop thinking and just let those rays of emotion rip through your heart. Let that sunlight shatter your thoughts, and may any fog of doubt evaporate in the light of rasa.

The Secret

[Bali]

The Balinese don't seem to age. More times than I can count, I've been awe-struck by the locals I've met who look 10, 20 years younger than their actual age.

Somehow, this does not surprise me. Just as Java had pure wisdom floating in its atmosphere, Bali seems to have... youth. Calm. Poise. Balance. It's no wonder people flock to this place to heal and rejuvenate themselves.

I asked one of my local friends, who is 38 years old and looks at least 10 years junior, what the secret to her youth was. She bursts out in giggles and says:

"The secret is always loving. Even your own stress."

It's so simple, isn't it? It always comes back to love. If you want to reverse aging, just love yourself... even the parts that you don't like. During my time here, the Balinese have taught me just how simple life can be in our pursuit for happiness. More to come…

Nakedness And Vulnerability

[Bali]

A recent experience in Ubud taught me a meaningful lesson on the power of nakedness and vulnerability. I went in for a Boreh treatment, a centuries-old healing recipe of herbs and exotic spices that are rubbed on the body. What the spa didn't tell me was that this required me to strip down completely naked, be lathered in the concoction, and then be bathed by the masseuse. .

Needless to say, it got intimate real quick. What took me more aback, however, was how the act of disrobing in front of a total stranger felt so natural. For a second I struggled to understand why, but then it clicked—I do this every day. Every day, I shed layers of myself in front of complete strangers.

This moment struck a deep chord because it was highly symbolic of everything I've been doing with my project to couchsurf around the world through my social network in the past few months: putting myself out there, raw and exposed, as I meet complete strangers who somehow always end up taking care of me.

Being hosted in a stranger's home is as intimate of an act as letting someone see you unclothed—perhaps that's why it enables host and guest to get close so quickly. There's something so vulnerable about fully entrusting yourself to someone else and giving that person power to hurt you with the faith that they won't.

Being vulnerable means allowing others to shape you, hurt you even. It's letting go of that fear and trusting that the world will take care. Don't be afraid to shed your layers... there's something transformative waiting in that sheer nakedness.

The Absurdity Of Freedom

[Bali]

I've always been enamored with the concept of freedom. I left New York for freedom. I travel for freedom. I have a hard time with commitment because freedom.

But really, what the hell is freedom?

As my host in Indonesia told me, "the term freedom is too absurd, extreme, and unclear." Why did I feel frustrated, he asked, when I was finally living this so-called freedom?

To which I blurted out: "even though I'm looking for freedom, I still feel like a slave."

It took me months to understand that freedom is not necessarily making away with commitments, being location independent, or having the ability to travel whenever. Freedom, I realized, is being okay with not knowing where you're going.

Those who hold onto that inherent need to "know" are ultimately enslaved by it. Not needing to know what's next—that utter comfort and acceptance of uncertainty—is what truly untethers us.

When there is lightness in your mind, there will surely be freedom in your heart.

Speak Your Dream

[Bali]

Since I set off to couch-surf around the world through my social network six months ago, I've experienced what I can only describe as tiny miracles every single day. There is not a day that passes without something magical, unexpected, or completely unbelievable happening. This includes meeting people who help me in the exact moment that I need it, privately asking myself a question that later gets answered by conversations with strangers, or witnessing one of the most beautiful sunsets I've ever seen.

Before arriving to Bali, I was on the verge of burnout from working super hard on making full-time travel a reality. I had to take a step back and seriously consider why I was pushing myself beyond my means.

Every day here, I've met people who have helped me understand that there is a magnetic energy that enables life to just "work out" when we are on the right path. It's inexplicable, unquantifiable, and cannot be harnessed. We either tap into it or we don't, and when we do, there is no need to try so hard because life just flows where it needs to.

When speaking to my new Indonesian friend about this, his response was: "Your word is your wish. Your wish is your dream. Your dream is your future."

Roughly translated from Indonesian, he meant: when you say you will pursue your dream and really mean it, it is only a matter of time before it comes true. Your word is the command that sets these tiny miracles into motion.

Simply put: when you have a dream that you believe in and take action towards fulfilling it, it ceases being a wish and starts becoming a reality. From there, everything works in your favor—even the challenges you face.

Speak your dream. Transform it from wish to reality, and watch the little miracles roll in.

We Know Nothing

[Bali]

Today I read that the opposite of knowledge is not ignorance—it is wonder. Wonder as in, the ability to absorb and feel something without feeling like you have to know why. Funny enough, travel is one of the few activities that somehow allows my hunger for knowledge and my need to feel void of it to live in perfect harmony.

One of the biggest lessons that I've learned during this journey around the world is that I know nothing. Most of my days have been passed in wonder, learning about different nooks of the world and the beautiful people that inhabit them. I've been awed by humans, nature, and culture alike. I've gone to places and been completely clueless as to what I was getting myself into and weirdly enough, I love how that makes me feel.

There is grace in accepting your ignorance and surrendering yourself to wonder. Standing in front of nature's phenomena and savoring just how tiny and meaningless I am next to it is but a reminder.

To acknowledge that I know nothing has made me receptive to the change that life consistently throws at me, because hey, who am I to know what blessings will come from it? The most profound transformation happens when you don't know what's coming next.

I know nothing, and I am better for it. That much, I know.

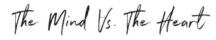

The Mind Vs. The Heart

[Bali]

I learned in Bali that there is a duality that lives within each one of us.

This duality is best described as that of the heart versus the mind. There are two forces at play in our psyche: what we want (the heart) and what we think we want (the mind). They don't always agree.

This is something I've personally grappled with throughout my trip: my mind has been responsible for orchestrating my travels, pushing me beyond what I thought I was capable of doing, and keeping me going even when I was ready to give up. My mind has been my savior, yet it has also been my worst enemy.

Sitting with locals in a village in Ubud, I was told that I don't respect my heart. I feed my mind excessively while leaving my heart starving for attention.

"How am I to feed my heart?" I asked.

"Happiness," they answered. So what is happiness?

"It is what you can feel without thinking.

... Can I suggest something? To feel happiness, do something meaningless."

To respect my heart means allowing myself to do something meaningless just because I enjoy it beyond thought. Our minds seek quantifiable targets, but our hearts have a vision. .

Allow your heart to feel what cannot be thought. Perhaps it is precisely in meaningless that we can find the meaning we need.

A Breath Underwater

[Gili Islands]

I took my first breath underwater a few days ago and it was exhilarating. The closest comparison I can make to the sensation of diving was that it was a form of meditation. As I drifted through this underwater planet, the only audible sound was that of my own breath. I felt present, focused, and aware of every little movement that stirred around me. More importantly, I felt safe.

I have a confession: I've always felt tremendous reverence for the water. I don't like swimming alone and I'm apprehensive of the open sea. I made a completely last minute decision to try scuba diving for one reason only–I inherently trusted the people around me.

I really believed I would panic as I entered the pool for my first training session, yet I was shockingly calm. I later wondered why, only to realize that it comes down to trust.

I've spent the last six months putting my well-being in the hands of strangers and still cannot believe how the world has taken care of me. This was no different: I could feel, at my core, that my instructor cared about my comfort and ease. My experience scuba diving helped me understand that a major component of conquering our fears is trust.

When you have trust–not only in others, but also in yourself–you can go above and beyond what you believed you were capable of.

Memorize With Your Heart

[Bali]

As my time in Bali comes to a close, a final story about protecting the balance between the heart and the mind:

I think a lot. To anyone who reads my stories, this comes to no surprise. As I sat in a village in Ubud with my hosts (who happened to be spiritual healers), I was told that I had to respect my heart, which always takes second place in the constant battle between logic and emotion.

"Stop collecting," they said about my incessant need to absorb more from life than my mind (and sometimes body) can handle. Life can be exciting, and we may want to live it to the fullest, but we need to give ourselves time and space to process and reflect on what we've experienced.

We memorize so much with the mind and not enough with feeling. Isn't it funny, for example, how many people know that a frog goes "croak croak," but wouldn't recognize its sound when hearing it in nature?

We learn, we memorize, but we don't listen with our hearts enough. My biggest lesson in Bali was, give the heart a chance to mull over what your mind experiences. For while the mind is an endless cascade of thoughts and ideas, the heart is the pool that patiently receives and connects it back into the flow of life.

Oceania

Australia

Metamorphosis

[Cairns]

I went to a butterfly sanctuary near Cairns today, where I learned about the process of metamorphosis that caterpillars must go through to become butterflies.

I suppose it is not something we often think about: how these tiny, hairy worms sprout those majestic wings whose beauty leaves us agape.

To begin its process of transformation, a caterpillar must shed its skin and create itself a cocoon. Inside this cocoon, the caterpillar… dissolves. It simply dissolves into a liquidy, organic mess that is only contained by the shell that encases it.

After a month of metamorphosis, the butterfly is ready to emerge. But it's not easy—first it must go through a 3-hour process to extract itself from the cocoon. This process requires the utmost focus and vulnerability: if the caterpillar is disturbed as it is emerging, its wings will never see the light of day.

This made me wonder—is metamorphosis only reserved for insects? That shedding of my old skin… I've felt it. The painful liquifying of my ego for the sake of transformation… I've felt that too. The slow, vulnerable process of growing into my new skin and learning to flaunt its majesty… it's been so difficult to relinquish the outdated pieces of myself, yet the wings I have grown because of those sacrifices have never taken me higher.

The pain of metamorphosis is always worth it.

You Only Need One Person

[Tasmania]

I was recently taking a walk with one of my Australian hosts. I saw a musician singing in the middle of the street, guitar case open for prospective tips. So I asked my host, who is a fellow musician:

"Why would anyone play music in public, only for some pocket change? Why get up in the morning for a public that most times doesn't even pay attention?"

To which he said: .

"We only need one person... that makes the music worth it."

Confused, I pushed back. If you're so passionate about something, shouldn't you be doing it just for yourself? Why the need to play for others?

To which again, he contested:

"If you have that gift, you have to give it. One person is just as good as 2,000."

It was then that I ceased to ask questions, because I understood. Just as that musician in the street plays in the hopes of giving the gift of his music to at least one passerby, I too write for myself with the hopes of inspiring at least one person.

It's true that if you have a gift, you should develop it for no one else but yourself. BUT—that gift is meant to be given, and if you can influence someone with it.... you've already made a change.

Tasmanian Dreams

[Tasmania]

A story about why I was initially drawn to Tasmania: when I was a little girl living in Italy, I loved cartoons. I had this insatiable wanderlust, but I didn't know it yet—at least, I didn't recognize it as such.

One of those cartoons was The Tasmanian Devil by Looney Tunes. I remember sitting in front of the TV, cross-legged on the floor, giggling and gaping in awe at this faraway land called Tasmania. I couldn't even place it on a map, but I vividly remember thinking to myself: one day I'm going to go there.

And now, 20+ years later, I'm here. Back then, Australia seemed like such a magical and inaccessible place. I never gave up on my dream to see the world, and today, I've seen so much of it because I feverishly held on to the awestruck wonder I'd felt as a child, watching distant worlds play in front of a screen.

Crazy how childhood dreams have the potential to materialize when you don't stop believing in them. When nourished, the power of our will can bring even the farthest of lands just a bit closer.

Darkness Into Light

[Tasmania]

During my visit to Tasmania, I walked through a tunnel in Mona Museum that felt so representative of how, consistently throughout this six-month journey traveling around the world, I've found myself walking out of darkness and into a brighter light.

This journey has taught me that there is always, always a light at the end of the tunnel. No matter what you're going through or how endless it may appear, everything is temporary.

Time does not discriminate, but that does not mean we have to become its victims. Keep walking forward, allow time to pass through you rather than against you. It is only when you reach the light that you'll understand the purpose that a period of darkness served in your life.

Cede Control

Australia gave me space. First, literally: it's not a very crowded country and the system (for the most part) runs smoothly and efficiently. More importantly, though, it gave me space to think, process, and just BE. I met incredible new people, opened up my heart, burned out, recovered, and began to piece together the many puzzle pieces that have been accruing over the past few months.

My biggest lesson in this country? Think of life as a river. It is powerful, unstoppable, and has its own rules, most of which we cannot understand (or only will with time). When that river comes at you, don't fight the current. Swimming upstream will only exhaust you. Rather, learn to go with the flow.

Accept that sometimes, there is only so much you can do. Life throws curveballs, many of which can be turned into opportunities. Whatever it brings you, cede control. Let it carry you where it may, because in the end, you will always end up where you need to be.

New Zealand

Moments Of Awe

Oh, the moments I have spent in complete and utter awe of this place. I've seen incredible nature before, but New Zealand is on another level. On a daily basis, I couldn't stop thinking about how small and insignificant I was in the grand scheme of things.

We humans are but little creatures in this vast world. Little specks waiting to be blown away at a moment's notice by the very forces we are destroying with our actions.

If we could only remember, every day, that we are part of something much bigger than us—which we will never comprehend. Would we then be able to wake up every day and see the world as majestically as we do in these sporadic moments of awe?

Untied Knots

The other day, I bought a bag of apples at the grocery store in Queenstown. A few hours later, I sat struggling to open the very same bag that I had closed myself. Frustrated, I exclaimed:

"Why do I tie knots that I can't untie?!"

My own question took me so aback that I stopped and laughed at myself. It's true, isn't it? Sometimes we tie knots so deeply that we ourselves don't know how to loosen them. Why DO we make things more complicated for ourselves than they need to be?

Life is much simpler than how most of us approach it, and most of that simplicity can be found by ceding control. There is no need to tie tight little knots to contain things just as we want them. Maybe the answer to leading a less complicated life is allow it happen as it should and let the apples fall where they may.

Courage Is A Muscle

[North Island]

People often ask me how I gathered the courage to leave everything behind to travel around the world, by sleeping on semi-strangers' couches nevertheless (I travel through my social network, which means everyone I stay with is loosely connected to me somehow).

I've learned that courage is like a muscle. Everybody has it, but for courage to strengthen within you, it NEEDS to be consistently exercised. The more you push yourself to perform small acts of courage, the more you'll be able to handle next time.

An act of courage is not jumping off a plane. It's walking into a stranger's home and trusting they will help, not hurt me. It's exposing my emotions, struggles, and most intimate thoughts to a public audience in hopes that my experience can help someone. It's as simple as telling people that I love them.

These are acts that compound and feed on each other, facilitating the next act. Believe in the courage that exists within you–it will unfold in ways you never thought possible.

Someone Else's Eyes

[North Island]

Sometimes while I travel, there is so much going on—and all happening so quickly—that I don't give the beauty around me the justice that it deserves. Shamefully, I become desensitized to it.

It's easy to get stuck in the entrails of our own vision and lose focus of what's in front of us. That's why I love to watch those I share my travel experiences with watch their surroundings.

Seeing wonder through someone else's eyes can be just as powerful as seeing it with our own: it is a reminder to look again, observe, and most importantly, to appreciate the world from a perspective other than our own.

Ultimately, it is not the places where I find myself that remind me of all the beauty that exists in this world—it is the eyes through which I see it.

Jumping Into The Unknown

[Wanaka]

I have many fears, but strangely, jumping out of a plane is not one of them.

As I sat in that plane, waiting to be launched into air from 15,000 feet above ground, I felt no trepidation. Rather, I was calm, serene, in place... similar feelings that arise when we find ourselves at home.

And so I jumped. As my perception shifted from looking up into the azure sky to seeing the planet unfold below me, there were no thoughts. Only a resounding "yes." In that moment, this is where I was meant to be. More so, this is WHO I was meant to be.

Fearless. Ready to jump. Unafraid of the unknown.

As I was free falling, suspended thousands of feet into the air, my first thought came to light: "Ah... of course." It made perfect sense, this feeling of being carefree yet secure, wise in my thoughtlessness, an active participant in the trajectory of my life while passively observing the uncontrollable.

I fell into a world that I've grown to become completely in love with, without knowing where I would land—and I was okay with that. This, to me, was freedom.

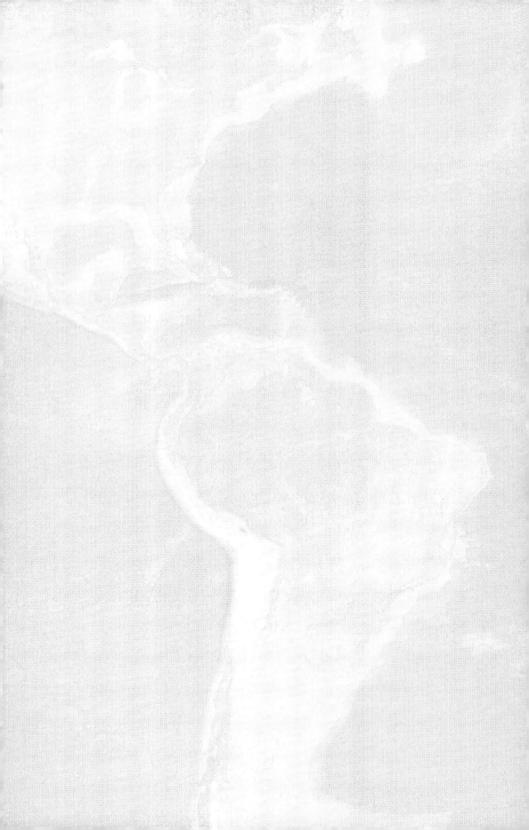

South America

Colombia

The Colombian People

What I love the most about the Colombian people is the way they pay attention to the tiny details that bring joy into their lives.

For the past 70+ years, Colombian history has been a tragic mess, with hundreds of thousands of deaths, 1+ million displacements, and other terrible violence committed by both the government and the guerilla/rebel groups.

Despite all the trauma they've had to deal with in their recent past, Colombians are some of the happiest people I've met. Their mindset has touched me deeply: rather than allowing shitty circumstances to bring them down, Colombians have a tendency to focus on the happiness of being alive.

As a local recently told me: "we Colombians take any happy moment and extract all the joy out of it in order to survive." When faced with adversity (in a place where violence was a day-to-day occurrence), they deal by turning the page: that is, dancing the night away, painting their homes in bright colors, joking around, warmly welcoming visitors, and living life as if there is no pain to grieve for.

"After a time, you learn to do that. Otherwise, you have to sit and cry." Thank you to the Colombians for showing me that, no matter what happens in our lives, happiness CAN be created. We are always capable of rising from our ashes.

The Art Of Forgetting

[Medellin]

I was recently speaking to a local about Colombians' impressive ability to celebrate and be joyous despite the many adversities they've faced (Colombia has struggled with violence and civil war for the past half century).

He responded: "Ah, yes. That's because Colombians are very trained in forgetting stuff."

Curious, I asked him what he meant, and his answer was telling. Colombia built quite the (negative) reputation during these many years of conflict. Scandals, violence, and corruption—especially during the "golden era" of drug trafficking—were such a regular occurrence that Colombians learned to deal with the humiliation and pain by quickly and collectively "forgetting" about the events. Despite all the terrible shit that's gone down in the past half century, you'll be pressed to find a Colombian who openly wants to talk about it, or "remembers" certain events.

Since then, the country has worked so hard to have positive things to be remembered for: for example, its hospitality, friendliness, joie de vivre, and beautiful landscapes.

The country has made a big effort to clean up its image and emphasize how much things have changed, and it shows. Even so, I am still conflicted on whether developing an attitude of intentional forgetfulness is the best way to go about it. I can't help but wonder: is it necessary to forget in order to overcome pain?

Our Worth

[San Andres]

I was chatting with a local about the socioeconomic situation in San Andres and what he said really struck me: "Money here doesn't make you a person. Your attitude does."

According to this local, social classes aren't as relevant in San Andres because everyone goes to the same places: since the island is so small, there are only a handful of hospitals, schools, etc that locals can pick from. Since everyone knows each other, the worth of a person is largely measured by how they treat their fellow islanders.

Whether this is true or not, I don't know, but isn't it a lovely thought that there are places that still value humanity over financial success? Money doesn't make you a better person; how you treat others is what will ultimately determine your worth.

Providencia

[Providencia]

There is only one main road in Providencia, and it circles the island.
The island is vastly untouched and underdeveloped, and most of its
population resides by the shores.

I found it quite captivating that you can go backwards or forwards on
this road, but you always end up in the same place. Time seems to be
suspended here, so it comes to little surprise that navigating the island
would take you right back where you started.

Farewell to one of my favorite places visited this year—may my path lead
me right back to you.

Facing My Fears

[Eje Cafetero]

I'm scared of riding horses. Being on top of a ginormous living, breathing body that has the power to crush or topple me in a matter of minutes frankly makes me quite nervous.

But tell me, is there a time you've conquered a fear and didn't come out better for it?

Various times per year, I find myself on a horse, riding in some foreign country along a beautiful landscape. Why?

Fear is a challenge, but it does not have to be an obstacle. I am faced with fears every day, yet I choose to look them in the face instead of running away. I may intimidated by horses, and yes, it's possible that something bad may happen, but realistically (and statistically), it won't.

If we filter our life experiences through unfounded beliefs that something will go wrong, we limit the possibilities of all that can go right. We cap our faith, serendipity, and the chance to discover parts of ourselves we previously didn't know existed. Not to mention, the very act of overcoming a fear prepares us to tackle the next (and bigger) one.

So I will continue to ride horses whenever the opportunity presents itself, and I will do so until the fear goes away. Fear is not meant to keep us in the shadow, but rather to push us into the light.

Ants On An Orange

[Cali]

Today I was having dinner with my Colombian host (and adopted "uncle"), who is in his late 50s and has extensively traveled the world. As he recounted fascinating stories of all the places he's visited, I curiously asked him how many countries he's been to. His answer shook me:

"I have no idea. It's one fucking world, what's the point of counting? We are like little ants walking on an orange."

When I asked him what he meant, he explained: "you see, you can travel the whole world and it does not mean a thing if you have not learned: we are nothing. And yet... we are everything. All we have is this life, and we have to enjoy it."

His comment reminded me that travel should not just be about tallying up countries or collecting cool dinner table stories. To me, travel is about developing the humility and goodwill to learn from all the different people I meet along the way. It is understanding my insignificance in this planet, yet still taking actions that will positively impact others. It is challenging myself to open my heart and live in the moment.

Ultimately, travel is not a matter of where I go or for how often, but rather how those experiences contribute to my growth. I don't need to see the entire world. I just want to feel it run through my veins.

Brazil

Love Is A Guiding Force

[Rio de Janeiro]

Today I met one of the most interesting people from my travels so far, a woman named Isabella.

Isabella was a victim of a Brazilian child trafficking ring in the 80s/90s, in which she was illegally ripped away from her mother and sold as a baby to a family in France. For years, she grew up in a turbulent family situation and disconnected from her roots, until she began questioning her reality and digging for the truth.

After returning to her home country of Brazil, she found out that many people (some who were supposed to protect her) were involved in this scheme. Even so, she seemed completely at peace when telling me her story.

I couldn't help but ask: how could she forgive these people? How does she not harbor hate in her heart for how others have betrayed and hurt her?

To which she told me: love is the only guiding force we have when it comes to living a happy life. She doesn't feel hate for people who do terrible things, but rather pity, because they've never experienced love.

Once you experience loving and being loved, you can't do that kind of evil. Because by truly feeling love, you understand that any hardship in life is conquerable when we have good people to support us through it. Anything can be accomplished when we have love for ourselves and those around us.

The Beauty Of Sunsets

[Rio de Janeiro]

A funny observation about watching sunsets in tourist spots: most people only stay until that little ball of fire drops into the horizon. After that... they leave. The show is over.

I recall some of the most beautiful "tourist" sunsets I've seen: in Santorini, Bali, and Rio de Janeiro. The venues would be packed with crowds of tourists, huddling against one another to take dozens of photos of the event. Once the sun sets, they give up: the venue empties, and everyone is off to dinner.

This has always puzzled me. In my experience, the true beauty of the sunset is not the ball drop so much as what happens shortly thereafter. It is when the sky lights up with shades of pastel and fire. In those quiet moments, when people think the show is over, God paints.

That exquisite beauty is too often neglected by those who are solely fixated on watching a sunset just to say they were there for it.

To me, it is not the event that is special: it's what comes after that holds the magic. It's not the birth, it's how the child is raised. It's not the proposal, it's how the marriage lasts. The sun sets every day, but the colors are never the same. Only some get to remain forever imprinted in your memory—but first you have to pay attention.

Where It Began:

USA

Hello America, Goodbye Me

[San Francisco]

After a long nine months abroad, I am finally back in mainland America. A lot has changed since then, but what's changed the most is myself. I am simply not the same person I once was. The Celinne who left New York City back in May is gone, confined to a shadow of who stands before my mirror today.

I return to the United States with a newfound knowledge of what it means to be human within a social network: 70+ hosts, 17 countries and 4 continents later, I've learned more about humanity and universal kindness than any story could recount. It almost feels foreign, to be sitting on this familiar soil turned inside out.

Hello America, and good-bye to who I once was.

Accepting Uncertainty

[San Diego]

Today I read a touching quote by Rumi about fear: "What is fear.....? Non acceptance of uncertainty."

Shortly thereafter, I read that it is love—not fear—that keeps you safe. We make so many of our decisions based off fear: of losing something, of failure, of not being good enough. We cannot stomach the uncertainty of not knowing how things will turn out because it makes us uncomfortable.

But what is there to fear, really? Fear doesn't keep us safe—it shelters us and blocks us from letting go. Yet, it is precisely by letting go that we develop acceptance, and it is through cultivating acceptance that we learn to love.

Whenever you are scared, remember to accept whatever it is that you cannot control. Do what you can, let the fear go, and invite love to flood in and fill that void.

Going With The Flow

[Honolulu]

Throughout my travels around the world, I am consistently reminded of what it really means to go with the flow. Theoretically, flowing should be an easy and smooth process–if you let it. But to most of us, flowing doesn't come naturally; we have to learn to find inner equilibrium within circumstances that are constantly shifting beyond our control.

Paddle yoga strangely taught me a lesson on what it means to go with the flow. When the wind blows you a certain direction, don't fight it–focus on feeling its breeze. When the ground shifts beneath your feet, remember to find your balance. When your surroundings feel strange and unfamiliar, ease yourself into them until they become comfortable. And never forget to occasionally dip your fingers into the water and feel the vast ocean that carries you.

Challenge yourself. Let the flow take you to where you need to be. You may fall off your paddle sometimes, but the good news is, you can always get back up.

Making Things Right

[Honolulu]

I recently learned about a fascinating Hawaiian concept called Ho'oponopono, which roughly translates to "the action of making it right." It is a practice of reconciliation and forgiveness: when something is out of alignment in your life, you need to not only understand what it takes to make it right but also take action towards it.

Back in the day, Hawaiian villagers would have small meetings for Ho'opono-pono to resolve their problems, which they believed caused illness if held in.

A native Hawaiian described the process to me in the most beautiful manner. Imagine that we are a bowl of light. Every fear, anxiety, and problem we have is a stone dropped in that bowl. We must continuously practice releasing those stones from the bowl to create harmony within ourselves, with others, and with the divine.

By helping one another let go of the stones through reconciliation and forgiveness, we create the necessary space for our light to shine brighter. Become a beacon of light to attract what you want in life, and never forget to use that light to illuminate that of others.

Purified Negativity

[Maui]

As I was browsing through a bookshop in Maui, I read a Tibetan saying that goes: "negative action has one good quality; it can be purified."

One of the things I love most about my nomadic lifestyle is the ways in which serendipity finds me and completely transforms my travel experiences from negative to positive.

Last week my phone spontaneously died and I almost lost thousands of photos/videos worth of content. While I was dealing with that very stressful situation, I made friends with the guy who fixed my phone. He happened to have a boat and invited me to go exploring.

Long story short, what started as a stressful experience led me to the best day I had in Maui: I snorkeled through the Hawaiian ocean, saw some amazing sea life like turtles and whales, listened to whales singing underwater, and most importantly, made some incredible new friends.

Nothing is negative in and of itself. You are capable of transforming any seemingly negative experience for the better. All you have to do is keep your mind and heart open to the unexpected.

Where Your Thoughts Go

[Maui]

When I was in Hawaii, a local Hawaiian woman said to me: "where your thoughts go, energy flows."

Your thoughts have energy. That energy changes not only how you perceive your life, but how your life treats you.

Think good thoughts, and your surroundings will manifest as such. The world that we experience is, after all, a reflection of who we have chosen to become.

An Alien In New York

[New York City]

It's been about two weeks since I've been back in New York City, and although being home feels comforting, it is also alienating.

I am walking down the streets of one of the most important cities in the world in my fancy clothes that I dug up from storage, but I am not the same anymore. The glamour of this city and the price tag of these clothes mean little to me now that I've understood that the things that most make me happy in life are intangible.

While I see the city playing out before me like a movie scene, I am no longer an actor. I am still not sure if that makes me feel outcasted, relieved, or even worse, indifferent.

This much I know: like people, places come in and out of our lives for a reason. We choose them because they are exactly what we needed for our growth in that moment. It may not feel the same to me, but New York is–and always will be–a reminder of the better, stronger, and wiser person that I've become.

The Meaning Of Friendship

[New York City]

What does friendship mean to you? I've found myself asking that question to dozens of people around the world, but not enough to myself.

I've realized, especially during this global circumnavigation trip, that true friendship is proven through action rather than words. Since I first left New York, I've observed people who I considered good friends drop off the map. Conversely, people I had previously overlooked (and even strangers) stepped up to the plate and supported me in ways I could never have imagined.

While I believe that people are inherently good, I also think that most don't understand the value of friendship. Perhaps modern age's over-abundant access to "friends" has cheapened the meaning. To me at least, friendship means shaping each other into better humans through unconditional support, going above and beyond to soothe your friend's pain, and intuiting that they need you before they even speak a word. At the very least, it is making someone's existence a little more meaningful by your presence.

Have you been a good friend? If not... why not start?

With that being said, I'd like to take a moment to appreciate the people who have most supported me during this journey. Thank you for always being there to pick up my calls, share tears and laughter with me, and having the wisdom and care to ask me "no really, how are you doing?" when everyone else assumed it was all dandy.

What Does It Mean To Stay?

[New York City]

For the past nine months, I've been asking myself the same question: where am I going next? My life revolved around deciding what places to visit, what I'd do there, and where I'd stay. Of course, this constant movement was more than just physical. Every day, my instability pushed me to evolve, adapt to change, and make the best of my fast-paced life.

Now that I have learned what it means to go, I am left trying to answer a completely different question:

What does it mean to stay?

To me, staying is much harder than leaving. While I've mastered the skills associated with picking up and moving forward, I have yet to feel comfortable staying in one place for too long. Perhaps this is because I associate staying with stagnation.

But this is not necessarily true. Staying can also foster patience, depth, and commitment. It can allow us to see more clearly what we are running from once the dust settles.

Staying is scary, but dare I say it has as much to teach me as leaving has?

What about you—what do you think "staying" means?

One Year Later

Today marks a special anniversary. Exactly one year ago, I left home with a carry-on and a one-way ticket. I had just quit my corporate job in NYC, and was attempting to circumnavigate the globe by couch-surfing through my human network—meaning everyone I stayed with was somehow connected to someone I knew in the flesh.

Fast forward to today, and I did it. Not only have I circled the world and stayed with almost a hundred people since leaving home (most of them strangers: my "loosest" connection was seven degrees!), I have made countless meaningful friendships, saw more of the world that I could have dreamed of, and made an unwavering commitment to myself to always remain faithful to my dreams.

After a year of 20+ countries, five continents, and first-hand witnessing the kindness of hundreds of strangers, I have changed in ways that words could never properly describe. Here is to another year of adventures, dream-chasing, and believing in the good of humanity.

Reflections
From The Other Side

Freedom Of Just Being

When I left my corporate job to travel the world last year, I thought I was finally free. I was wrong. My mistake was equating not having a job to show up to, rent to pay, or a system to answer to as freedom.

A few months into my journey, I was commenting to one of my hosts that, despite finally being unchained and free to do as I pleased, I still felt unfulfilled. When he asked me why, the words effortlessly blurted from my lips: "Even though I'm looking for freedom, I still feel like a slave."

At the time, I couldn't understand why I felt this way, but now I do.

A teacher recently told me, "You can't talk or think your way to freedom. It's experiential." Freedom cannot be attained by a lack of commitments, money, or free time. Sure, favorable external conditions help tremendously, but like happiness, ultimate freedom can only come from within.

The very thought of "how do I find freedom" imprisons us in an endless chase, looking for something that cannot be found and preventing us from fully experiencing the present.

All along, the answer was right here, in the now: freedom is the ability to just be, without needing to know what's coming next.

Trust Your Instinct

A question I get asked all the time is: aren't I scared of meeting and staying in the homes of strangers when I travel?

This answer may feel fluffy, but it's the honest truth: I'm not scared because I trust my instinct.

First, interacting with and reading the behavioral patterns of hundreds of people while on the road has taught me to discern when people have good intentions. Second, I'm a strong believer in the law of attraction: you attract what you are. I try to approach most of my interactions with kindness, good intention, and helpfulness, so that is how I believe people will behave towards me. And usually, it is.

A Balinese villager once told me: "Your heart cannot be fooled. It always knows what's right. When you have a good heart, you will know if people are good or not." When someone has bad intentions, I can "feel" something is off and I instantly take actions to remove myself from the situation. The point being: be smart, take care of yourself, but don't assume that people are out to hurt you because that is the world you'll create for yourself.

Trust your intuition. You are your best savior.

Here's To Another Breath

One year after my visit to Nepal, I spent a week in a silent meditation retreat in Massachusetts. There, I met a man with cerebral palsy whose aura shone with a light that's hard to find these days. Though at first it was difficult to understand him, I sat through it and tried to really be present and listen. Minutes before my silence began, he offered me profound advice that I will carry with me always.

Do not take the meditation, he said. Let it take you. Don't stress if it's not going according to expectations because, as he nonchalantly added: "Every breath is a second chance."

I don't think he himself realized the gravitas of his words. They plunked into my heart with a thud, almost startling me with their significance. What a simple concept, yet so meaningful all the same: we can always start again.

Every moment brings with it a new opportunity to fix our mistakes, to try again, to apologize, to love, to be present for someone and for yourself. It's never too late. Each breath we take carries with it a new opportunity.

Today is the day you get to start living a life that fills you with pride. Keep breathing and keep trying, so long as the air flows through your body.

Hurt A Few Times. Love A Thousand

Last year, I walked into a café in a tiny Greek island two hours from Santorini, and I asked the owners for a place to stay that night.

Just the day prior, I had spent the day with a Santorini local (also a recently met stranger), who—after hearing I was traveling there and didn't have a host—recommended that I visit and trust these people.

I ended up being hosted for four days by one of the owners, a middle-aged Greek local man, who was one of the gentlest souls I'd met during my social experiment couch-surfing around the world.

Had you asked me if I would have dared to walk into a shop and ask a stranger for a couch to sleep on just a few months prior to that day, my answer would have been "never."

You see, I doubted that people were good.

I doubted that people would help me follow my dreams.

I doubted that people would keep me safe.

I was wrong.

And I don't say that because I read it in a book or someone told me about it.

I lived it.

Since I left New York City in May of 2016, I've put my faith and well-being at the hands of over a hundred strangers.

From experience, I've learned that:

- When given the opportunity, people want to be good

- When you give trust, you receive it

- When you love with an open heart, the Universe takes care of you

Call it optimistic, if you will. But I'd rather be optimistic and get hurt a few times, than be pessimistic and not love a thousand.

Every Drop Counts

One of my favorite quotes of all-time is from the book Cloud Atlas and it goes, "My life amounts to no more than one drop in a limitless ocean. Yet what is any ocean, but a multitude of drops?"

These words beautifully represent a life paradox that I subscribe to: we are nothing and everything at the same time. It's hard to accept, but it's quite possible that every action that we take in our lifetime will be forgotten. In the grand scheme of things, our minuscule existence represents little more than a drop in the ocean.

Even so… our actions DO have consequences. Every action we take has a ripple effect somewhere in the world. We can't possibly predict who our actions will impact or inspire, but rest assured that someone out there will be affected by your decisions.

The real question is—what do you want to make of this life? Do you want to live it solely for yourself, or do you also want to contribute to the well-being of the planet during your short time here?

Collectively, everything we do matters, but only if we are each chipping in our part to contribute to the whole of humanity. Together, we are as powerful as the ocean.

I can only hope to honor my responsibility in this world, while staying humble to my insignificance.

Replenishing The Heart

I spent a year putting my well-being in the hands of hundreds of strangers, first-hand witnessing their kindness and willingness to help me along my journey. The experience cracked my heart open and, for the first time, I allowed people to freely take from it.

But what about replenishing the heart when it's tired? What happens when there is giving, but receiving is hard?

That is what I'm learning now: to give love unconditionally, you must also be open to receiving it.

What does it mean to give love? Wearing kindness in your eyes. Being willing to help someone when they are in need. Exercising compassion for and standing by people's vulnerabilities, so they remember that they are loved, accepted, and wanted.

But then, there is the question we don't ask ourselves enough... what does it mean to receive love? It is looking in the mirror and wearing that same kindness. It is listening to your own needs and being willing to help yourself. It is knowing to take a step back when that heart is feeling depleted, because you, too, are vulnerable and human.

We are taught to give more than we receive, and to an extent that is true. But that does not negate the absolute necessity of receiving love. That's what gives us the energy to give to others. The root of true love, in the end, is ourselves.

Do Your Part

I'm frequently asked how I live a life that enables me to travel full-time, pursue my passions, and enjoy my days and the incredible humans around me to the fullest.

The answer: living your dream begins with MINDSET.

When you want something with all of your heart, the Universe works in your favor, but first you have to allow yourself to want it. Once that happens, you create a clear vision of what your dream is, and consistently take action towards it until your physical world becomes a manifestation of the passion that you hold inside. That's how life design happens. And that's how dreams come true.

First, decide you want the dream.

Then, envision it clearly.

Lastly, take action every single day to move your dream from thought to reality.

Do your part, and the Universe will do the rest.

Listen To Your Intuition

When I arrived to Bali last year, I felt broken. At that point, I had been traveling nonstop for six months and had completely burned out from the physical, mental, and emotional exhaustion.

I didn't anticipate how much energy this would take out of me. I was running out of money, I hadn't seen friends or family since I left, I was sleeping in the homes of stranger after stranger, and on top of that, I was also working and trying to figure out what to do with my life once I finished my circumnavigation.

Then, I came to Bali, and it healed me.

Specifically, the Balinese people did. I spent my days here with locals who, through their wisdom and Indonesian philosophy, taught me a lesson that I will hold with me for life: to respect my heart.

In the pursuit of our dreams, obstacles are inevitable. We will fatigue, exhaust, be on the verge of giving up even. Our mind will ask us to do more, do it better, so we can be good enough. But it's not our mind we should be listening to.

It's our heart.

Listen to what your intuition tells you. Approach your obstacles with love and acceptance. Allow the kindness of others to guide you. Most importantly, take care of yourself when you need it.

Since my first visit to Bali, I began respecting my heart, and I kept going.

One year later, I am here again, and my life has transformed in ways that I couldn't have anticipated... for the better.

The Meaning Of Meaninglessness

When was the last time you did something meaningless?

Last year in Bali, I learned a lesson about happiness and following your heart that I'd like to pass on.

There is a duality that lives within each one of us. This duality is best described as what we want (the heart) and what we think we want (the mind). They don't always agree. Sitting with locals in a village in Ubud last year, I was told that I excessively fed my mind while leaving my heart starved for attention–consequently neglecting what I truly wanted.

"How am I to feed my heart?" I asked.

"Happiness." They told me, "It is what you can feel without thinking." So, what can we do to feel more happiness?

Their answer: "Do something meaningless."

Happiness sometimes means allowing ourselves to do something meaningless just because we enjoy it beyond thought.

What do you like to do that's meaningless but brings you joy? For me, it's watching clouds and a starry sky. Allow your heart to feel what cannot be thought. Perhaps it is precisely in the meaningless that we can find the meaning we need.

Trust Impermanence

Today is my 27th birthday. Exactly two years ago, I spent the entire day choking back tears at a corporate New York City job I was utterly unsatisfied with, after being unexpectedly dumped the night prior by a man I wasn't crazy about.

One year ago, I was six months into a journey around the world, a social experiment I had designed in which I circumnavigated the globe by staying with locals I met through real human connection.

I had just arrived to Bali, and I was alone and burned out. Even so, I knew in my heart that I was on the right path. I spent that birthday surrounded by friendly strangers, who barely knew me but made me feel right at home.

Today, I am in Bali once again, surrounded by friends who I love and cherish. I have never felt so happy, fulfilled, and on track with my life as I do now and I don't even have it all figured out. I have been on the road for 1.5 years and have no idea when I am stopping. I'm still confused AF about a lot of stuff.

And that's okay.

I am living my dream, and evolving it every single day.

I've learned that challenges, obstacles, and struggles are transient. They come and they go, but what stays is your conviction that you are living a life that you love.

Trust impermanence.

It will bring you surprises (some pleasant, some not), it will make you nervous, it will make you feel like you're balancing on a string, but so long as you listen to your heart and hold your vision, you will get to exactly where you want to be.

Thank You Universe for another year of life, for teaching me what it means to feel happy and fulfilled, and for the blessings I receive each and every single day. Thank You for the hundreds of incredible, wise, and kind people that have guided me along my path since I took my leap of faith. Most importantly, thank You for bringing me back to myself.

To All The Dreamers

I've often wondered why dreamers give up. There are so many reasons for why we may not see our dreams through: we are too scared, we don't feel like we are good enough, or perhaps we distance ourselves so much from our vision that we feel like it's time to move on or grow up.

Following your dreams is really fucking hard–I'm trying every day and I have days I just want to break. But in the end, even after all the ways that the pursuit will challenge and test you, it is worth it.

I've never felt so alive, truer to myself, and bound to a higher purpose than when I've allowed my heart to guide me. Who says that dreams and reality must inhabit separate realms?

This is for all the dreamers–stay more passionate than your pain, believe in your madness, and fuel the conviction that, despite what the rest of the world says, your dreams are indeed at your fingertips.

An Open Letter To My Hosts Around The World

To the 70+ kindred spirits who opened their home to me during my journey:

Back in May of 2016, I decided to leave behind my corporate life in America to pursue a passion project: I wanted to circumnavigate the world by couch-surfing through my social network. As you well know, the caveat to this project was that I could not use the website: everyone who hosted me had to be connected to me somehow.

I was admittedly quite nervous when I got on that one-way flight to Italy. Could I really find people willing to host me, everywhere I went? Would they even be open to welcoming a complete stranger into their home?

The answer? Yes.

I want to let you know that because of you, I've just done what less than a year ago I deemed impossible. Words cannot ever encapsulate what you've done for me by collectively taking turns welcoming me into your home.

So, thank you.

For you, this was an act of kindness. You asked me for nothing in return. You sheltered me, fed me, let me use your washing machine, drove me around, showed me the city you live in through your unique and local perspective. You asked me about my project and my life. You encouraged me when I expressed doubt. You poured your heart out to me when I shamelessly prodded you with my endless questions. You were my cheerleader when I was exhausted and on the verge of giving up.

You went above and beyond providing the couch I asked of you—I still chuckle thinking about the host who boiled me water so I didn't have to take a cold shower in the middle of a thunderstorm, the ones who woke up at the crack of dawn to drive me to the airport, the one who flew up 1,000 miles so I wouldn't have to road trip down to his city alone, or the one who spent hours calling tourism agencies to arrange proper transportation in a very complicated 3rd world country.

Most importantly, you believed in me, and by doing that, you helped me believe in myself. When I think about the steps that I am taking to pursue

my dream to travel the world full-time, my heart explodes with gratitude upon recognizing that each one of you has laid down a stone to pave my way.

Perhaps if I had only visited your city, and stayed with you, this wouldn't have left as deep of an impact. But holy shit, there were over seventy of you. The fact that I've been able to circumnavigate the globe by staying with locals (mostly strangers) makes this a very big deal. People like you are why I have unshakable faith that we are all capable of pursuing our dreams, that we each have the opportunity to accomplish great feats if we help each other out just a little bit. You are why my heart has grown tenfold since I left my life in New York City. You've proven to me that when we believe in ourselves, and have the support of other people who believe in us too, our potential is limitless.

The gift you gave me is much, much greater than those few nights in your home. You've renewed my hope for humanity, and shown me generosity and kindness to an extent that I did think existed until I witnessed it with my own eyes. You've inspired me more than ever to pay it forward to others who need help. You've taught me that hope can be served in the simplest of dishes (those homemade fried spring rolls and grilled venison being some of my favorites), and that I can be equally satisfied and fulfilled sleeping on a shabby couch in a small apartment as in a king-sized bed in a penthouse.

It was never the "couch" that mattered: it was you. It's the precious human connections that we've made on the sole commonality that we are both people trying to find our way in this vast world. Somehow, for reasons beyond explanation, we found each other. And even if we never see each other again (which I hope is not the case!), you've touched and influenced my life in ways that will ripple through time. A single thread of love binds us, one that is intricately woven into the fabric of our collective hopes and dreams. I feel forever connected to you, and you will hold a special place in my heart for what you've done.

I ask of you one last thing: keep doing what you do. Spread your luminous self to the world, because I can attest that even if your kindness felt like a small action to you, it has changed my life. Who knows how many others you can influence.

From the deepest crevices of my heart... thank you.

Love,

Celinne

About The Author

Celinne Da Costa is a brand identity and storytelling coach, published writer, and active dreamer, building her business and exploring from wherever in the world she chooses to be. Sounds like a dream, right? It is, but that's because she designed her life that way.

Celinne was born in the heart of Rome, Italy, to an immigrant Brazilian mother and a German-raised Italian father. Since leaving Italy seventeen years ago, she's gone from living in the quintessential Connecticut suburbia that American dreams are made of, to studying in one of the country's Ivy League schools, University of Pennsylvania, to spending a few years stuck in a cubicle of one of New York City's most prestigious advertising agencies.

In 2016, Celinne left her unfulfilling corporate marketing career in New York City to become the architect of her own life. This meant crafting a story that allowed her to infuse every day with meaningful moments of human connection, internal space for self-discovery, and opportunities to pursue her passions... all while seeing the world.

Her mission is to create a life story that is full of joy, meaning, and purpose—and to help others do the same, so they can feel more empowered to pursue their dreams and enrich their lives with real, human connections.

Celinne contributes to and has been featured in major publications around the world, including Forbes, HuffPost, Intrepid, Urban Adventures, Matador Network, Rosetta Stone, and Business Insider. She's helped clients in 20+ countries tell their stories, and has a loyal community of 40,000+ dreamers following her work and journey around the world. So far, she's traveled to 50+ countries and has no plans of stopping.

Visit Celinne at www.celinnedacosta.com.

Follow her journey on Instagram, Facebook, and Twitter @ CelinneDaCosta.

This is what I live for:
the sheer wonder of knowing nothing,
yet feeling everything.

Made in the USA
San Bernardino, CA
18 February 2018